Marcellus M. Menke

THE ENGLISH POEMS
OF AN UNKNOWN
GERMAN POET

AF175553

Marcellus M. Menke

THE ENGLISH POEMS
OF AN UNKNOWN
GERMAN POET

POEMS

editionHIC<

Marcellus M. Menke
The English Poems of an Unknown German Poet
Poems
Illustrated with 13 digital drawings by Michael A. Holst

2nd Edition, Cologne 2022

Layout, cover design and typesetting: Marcellus M. Menke
marcellus.m.menke@m4art.de

Bibliographic information of the German National Library:
The German National Library lists this publication in the Deutsche
Nationalbibliografie; Detailed bibliographic data are available on
the Internet via dnb.dnb.de.

Production and publishing: BoD – Books on Demand,
Norderstedt

ISBN: 9783756859467

for you

I. Excuses

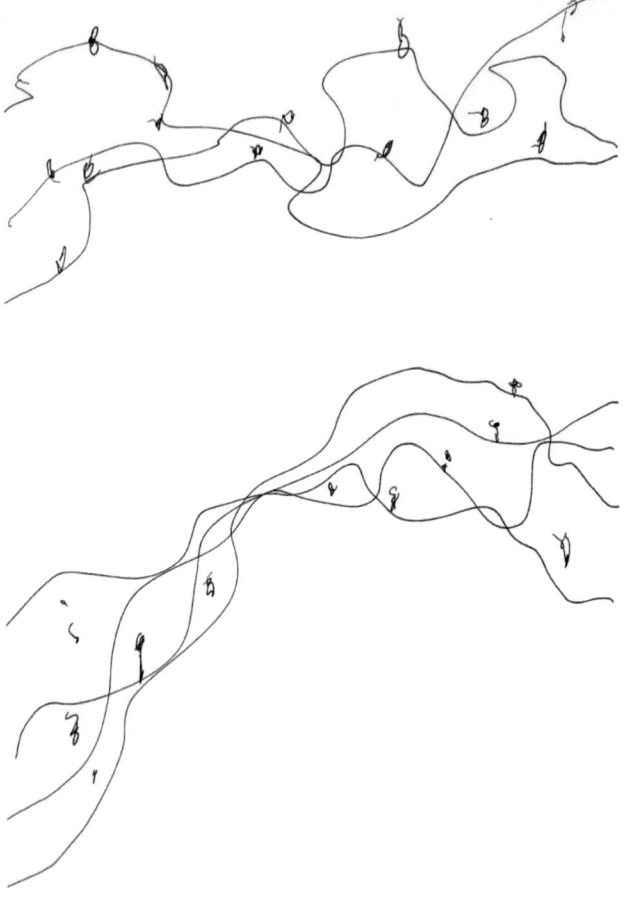

Michael Holst: Landscapes Cloudfusing
Digital Drawing 2022

Heard

I have heard
of some amusingly
irregular words.
They behaved in a way
no one expected
and their behavior
was the cause
of some unpredictable
trouble
no one thought of.

You may say
that looking
on some pages
of my old
school book grammar
may have prevented
this.

broken garden

my english [thoughts]
[are] (is) a broken garden
of empty envelopes

Indeed

It may be
indeed
a little bit
late
for an excuse
or a change
or for
both
and perhaps
even a big excuse
and a great change
won't be able
to change
the expected disaster.

It already is there.

But of course
there is
still
the possibility
to make it
less
worse.

The question is:
can we change?

PS.: I love the world.

The limitations

The limitations
of the summer rules
may not be acceptable
and who knows
if it was right.
But of course
you today
don't know
whose mistake
you are making
may be or not.

Falling

When black drops
on my face
are straightly
falling down
from the middle
of my nose
and memory
starts to wane.

It may be
the moment
when the
English poems
of the unknown
German poet
start to stammer
a little bit
too much
to be still
understood

You at least
mad a try,
had a try.

Poetry

English poems
of a German
unknown poet
about stars
and their dust
some plutonium particles
deep in the ocean
and the story
they tell about
the history
of our universe.

And somehow,
for a moment or two,
focusing to the lines
of the book
about the history of books*
saying
that it may be
one of the often unknown
or not taken into account
facts,
that most books
are or stay
unread,
as the book with this poems
probably will be too.
But that should not
be the criterion

that makes this book
a book.

*The Oxford Illustrated History of the Book, Edited by James Ra-
ven. Oxford University Press 2020, ISBN 978 0 19 870298 6

II. Expectations

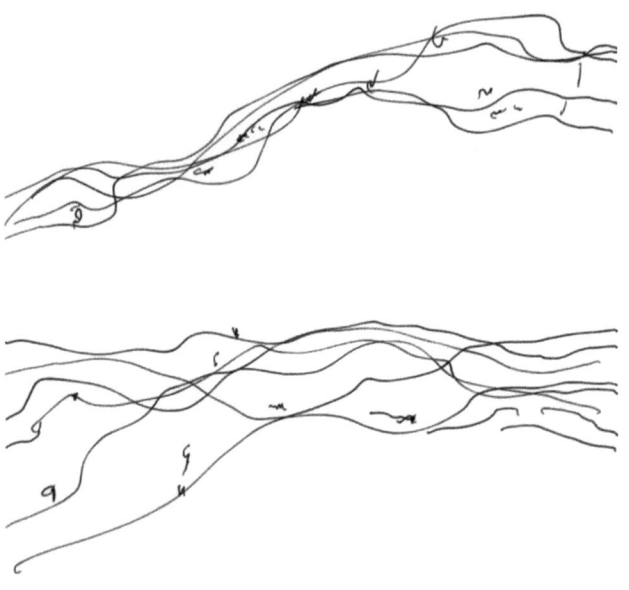

Michael Holst: Landscapes Study 7.879.542
Digital Drawing 2022

In the glow of the night

In the glow of the night
I make up my mind
for the days to come
for the hours and weeks
I want to expect
as a gift
as an encounter
of given grace:
My exercise to love.

Small

When the small particles
from the surface
floated away
they made me focus my view
in an before unknown direction.

Possibly I thought
that the world
was new
or got lost,
but neither
was the case.

Maybe the more adequate answer
to the not yet uttered question
would be
that it just was another period
in the so beautifully long chain of periods
of the swinging anthem of atoms.

But that may be
too pathetic.

Yes?

Last Summer's Papers

Last summer's papers
lie on my floor
or on the desk
and in my mind
the thoughts
that the floor, the ground
on which we stand
on which I stand
is the desk, the writing desk
on which I work, have to work
should work.

It is my (working-)space
this world
here.

III. Somewhere else

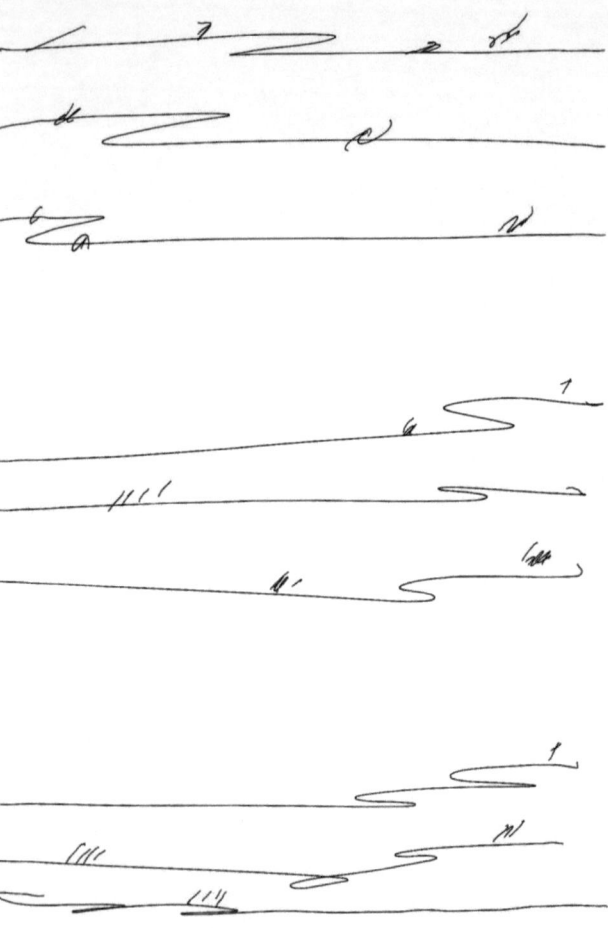

Michael Holst: Three Landscape Studies on a Windy Morning
Digital Drawing 2022

The fridge

The fridge
is my friend.
I can't talk to him
but he talks to me.

In the second
cycle of madness,
when everything
becomes warmer and warmer
the single hotspots
need reliable companions.

The fridge would be a good one
my presidential friend thought.

Moon light

The Moon was
a little bit too tired
to shine today.

It was said
that this had already
happened earlier.
But today
there obviously
was an unignorable utterance
and understanding was expected
from some sites.

It of course was
– that was what everybody thought –
about the humans
and their plans
to trample once again
on his surface
and there still was a
parking car left
having no ticket
for now over 50 years.

Er schien dann   It then shone
aber trotzdem   but anyway
und wunderschön.   and very beautifully.

26

Bear

Peter is praying
and David is praying
and the old watch
lying on the desk
counts the seconds
of the passing minutes
with its constant ticking
of the elapsing world.

Who is listening?

The bear
was brought
to a new church
though no one knew
what a bear
should do
in an church.
But the people
who organised it
thought that the
bear should know.

But later on
they found out
that he didn't know anything.
He even had forgotten
how to survive
and that made a church

a good place to be
for him
said Peter, finishing his prayers
and David laughed with a smile.

Dorningham Hill

In Dorningham Hill
there were discussions
about a survival strategy
for mankind and
some other creatures
on this little planet.

Some years later
still the same questions
were urgent
and no one understood
why the Dorningham Papers
were still secret.

My question is:
Would it make a difference
if they would be published?

The answers are known,
already for a long time
and realizing that there never
has been a Dorningham Declaration
shows that all discussions
today are only shadow-boxing
of people who don't want to act.
They simply don't want to do
what has to be done
because they are not willing

to give up their
single-sided partial profit
for the benefit of all
and that would
include them too.

Als wenn eine Katastrophe
nicht stattfände
wenn man so lebt
als gäbe es sie nicht.

As if a catastrophe
would not take place
if you live
as if it would not exist.

Thoughts

You may be called an undistinguished banana
or an apple fallen apart,
but the drowning pleasure may be
– for a short time –
removed.

Bitterns and wealth may be the
syllabled sisters or uttered brothers
of a fearful generation,
calling the trees their mothers
and the earth a father.

Let me not admit advanced
forms of understanding
to anyone reading these lines.
Let me not try
to see knowledge or understanding
in the striving or the denial of dreams.

Future

The stolen parenthood was no longer to hide
and the children admitted their fear
of being burned in the fire
of the expanding sun.
No one knew the shapes
and the riddles
thought as solved
were not even understood.
It is
only a small
period of time
a humans lifetime
and even the period of the earth's existence
is only an eyes blink.
But what is man
that he can understand this
or at least
gets near the area
where understanding could start?

IV. Reflections

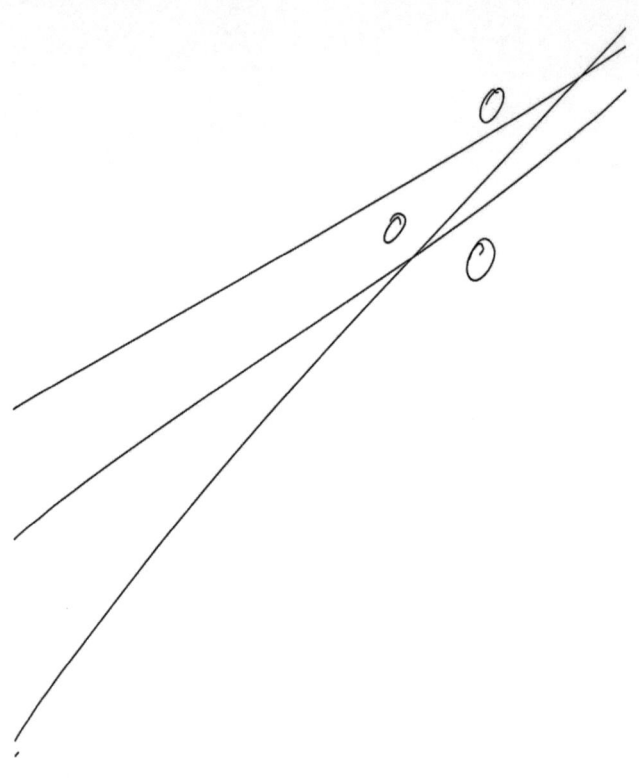

Michael Holst: Three Lines and Three Circles
Digital Drawing 2022

The old actor's dialogue

I am the man
who lives in the stolen
rose garden,
who's face
is a playing puppet
and who's soul
is lost
in noisy seas
of director's advice,
not knowing who I am.

I am the man
with the face
stolen so often
and I never
will get it
back.

I am the king,
the murderer, the beggar,
the gentleman, the lover or
the tragic dying hero.
And looking in the mirror
I only see the characters
I never see myself.

They stole
my face.

Broken

Broken rules
of unknown content
in a midlife swinging circle
following an unseen line
of single emptiness

Dreamcast

Following
some guideline questions
at tomorrow's meeting
eventually hidden
when asked about
the forms of love.

Your face won't flash
as it did in former times.
Too much
you got used
to the told stories
of excuse
and too common
your feel secured
behind the securing wall
hiding the untellable.

How open are my words
how honest are my lies
when they tell the truth?

Development
<or> The copy of the evolution
<or> How I make art

. (it all starts with a dot, of course)
first, of course
it simply is a copy
then it turns to an
understood copy
and finally it becomes
something new
that has not been
there before.

Pouring out

You feel the summer
pouring out on an
elaborated time scale,
the humid dustingly
shining air of the night
and the will understood
nothing, waiting for
good dreams.

It was

It was
the mother
of our prayers
that was left
in the small space
between the mountains' hills
left at the crossing
so accurately drawn
on the little electronic map
on the small device in front of you.

You should have
lovely memories,
is the thought
and perhaps this is
the only to be expected to stay
if after all anything will stay at all.

Please stay
is a voice I hear
and I want to be heard.

Will I still know
what these words meant
to me, while I wrote them,
when I read them again
in a few days?
Certainly not
I think

and continue my
interrupted night sleep,
thinking that of course
it was not a good idea
to read the newspapers
so early.

Easy

It is so easy
to write a romantic
poem about the moon
but it is so hard
to understand
the really true feelings
and even knowing
the difference between
imaginative and projected feelings
it is still a question
and the answer could be wrong.
And only knowing it
will be good for not
going wrong.

God dammed

The
god dammed
chicken eater
was so tired
so tired
so lost
in the
dark
that surrounded
him.
It was awful
the place
and in his mind
the dark snake
and the sinister clouds
and no way
to get
out.

A chicken
could be helpful
in this situation
not to eat
but to follow.
Chickens fly
if they are alive,
so let them stay
alive,
though too much

of them
make an awful
manure.

Language confusion

The stool was empty
and the summer
surprisingly
had finally reached
the end of the bed corners
especially the left corner
right behind.

On the floor
– a classical –
flowers
or the leaves of them,
but that was only a picture
in a book she never read.

My modest tries
to build a bridge
of understanding
was not at all
successful.
The rain was missing
hidden in clouds
we couldn't see.

Brains collection
of foreign words
incoherently emerging

Giving some praise
to a suddenly rising suburban landscape
on a lawn full of irritating lies.
There may be an urging future
and no one able or willing
to tell history in the daily-stories
around you, and someone else
may think the tears are
regrettably lying on the hidden
piece or part of a table
we all are sitting in front of.

No one knows
what disadvantages
made Peter Miller
– the unknown –
fly like a bat
in a laundering room
of a 19th century apartment
facing accommodation
on a small green and blue planet
in an extraordinary solar system.

There are no boundaries
to the words and the confusion
they may cause and show.

So being inadequately
hungry after a meal
that never
took place
at a garden party
may be an
explanation
never accepted,
thought
it may not be sure
that this isn't true
from some point
of view
and that is the view
that can or will
be changed quickly.

Try to leave,
these thoughts
may not lead to
a sufficient result.

The stolen language

Lost behind some bottles
in the kitchen's corner,
left behind for some time
waiting to recover
but at the end
simply lost.

And sadly
nobody is looking for
the lost words.

<9:00>

The brushes of gold
lie on the silver
moonlight memories
forgotten in the sky's lines
finding some rest
on the small mountain's
edges.

English saying № 673
of the unknown German poet

Grownups in the winter
are the summer's middle past.

Sweets ...

... are no solution
for a lonely
couple
of days.

No one wants
to look up
the steering list
of unknown words
steadily increasing.
And in the bubble
of the present unknown
words confusion
is growing as the
predominant world-
model.

Welcome to the club.

APPENDIX:
The last year
has been so exiting
that in July I already
have Silvester-feelings.

Roasted

Probably I wouldn't
be able at all
to eat the roasted doves
and the sparrow in the hand
certainly not

The last of the summer tales
has not, yet not, been told
and a shivering cat
hiding behind a wardrobes crown
is not the answer
to my questions.

The bombs
of Anna Karenina's successors*
certainly are not
an answer to the question
how to survive
in a struggling world.

---

*Carmen Boullosa: The Book of Anna, Coffee House Press 2020, ISBN 978-1-56689-577-4

The morning

glow in my eyes
and a reminder
of the fading
thoughts of the night
on the outer lines
of my lips

Not very well

I dreamed of a chocolate horse
I heard a voice saying
unknown time and place
and why should there someone dream
of a horse
made form chocolate
I asked myself
and thought of the dentist.
Zero times in behavioral psychology.

V. Bitter

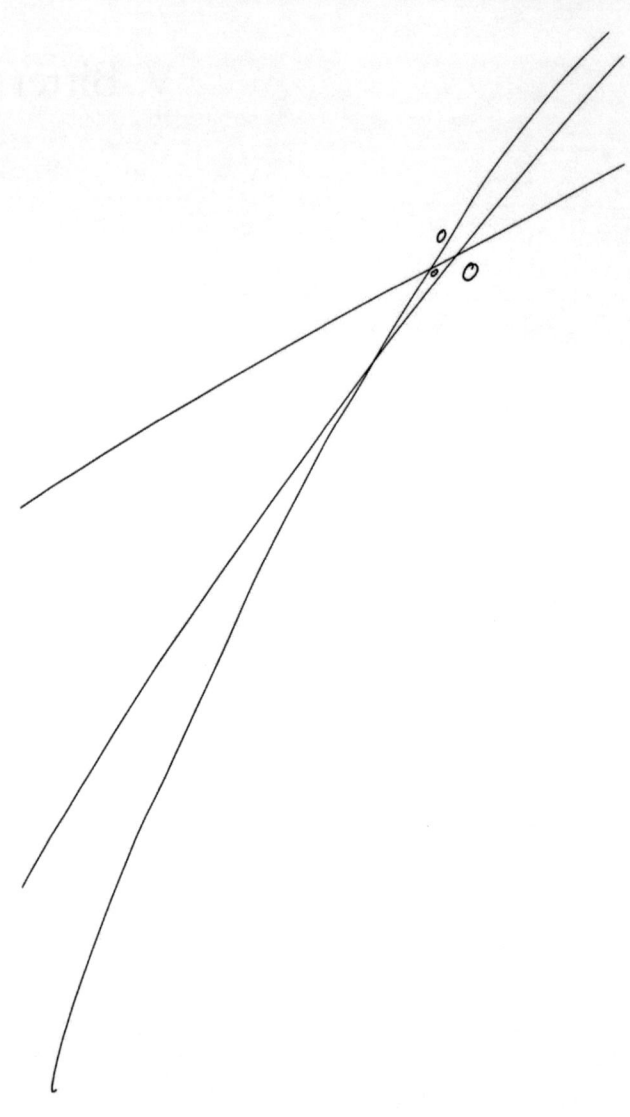

Michael Holst: Three Lines Ruled World
Digital Drawing 2022

Buried

The new worlds
of the past
lie buried
in the uncertainty
of the, like an ancient
thunderstorm rolling over,
future.

The payments
aren't done
and with
black and white
pixels on the wall
we don't understand
our job to do.
The emergency rooms colors
are spreading around the world.

Bittersweet cake

The fox was at the manger.
In the traditional tales
he was not there.

[I left out the rest]

The bitterness

the unfelt bitterness
of an unsold sweet
in a construction of a sweet shop
that seems not to fit
in a story I perhaps
haven't jet understood
may turn in a sewing shop
where the little fine needles
are used by well trained
little fingers sewing
used skirts to be used again.

But it may be the bitterness
that may stay
and maybe that is
the not so wrongly understood
author's intention

[APENDIX 1]
.. and me struggling in
blurred pictures
in an only approximately
understood foreign language.

[APENDIX 2]
In my mind
– once again –
the question
why I have the

unprovable believe
having more understanding
of Russian's 18th century literature
than a recommended
Spanish speaking author,
as my knowledge is
only from the
German translations

[APENDIX 3]
And now time
for the second
morning sleep

[APENDIX 4]
Mixed up
sweat [Schweiß]
sweet [Süßigkeit]
sweat shop [Ausbeutender Betrieb]

Welcome on
the glorious road
of misunderstandings.

---

*Thoughts while reading the first chapter of Carmen Boullosas "The Book of Anna". ISBN 978-1-56689-577-4.

Drops

A side drop
for a paragraph
of
freedom,
read between the
carefully drawn lines
on the irritated map.

The bottle

The bottle in the wardrobe
empty bottle in overcrowded wardrobe
straight expired
and frankly not
in the right
measurement department.

Change.

The possible change
and the really taking place
and the feared
and the expected
developments …

Mind the gap
wherever it is.

VI. Hope

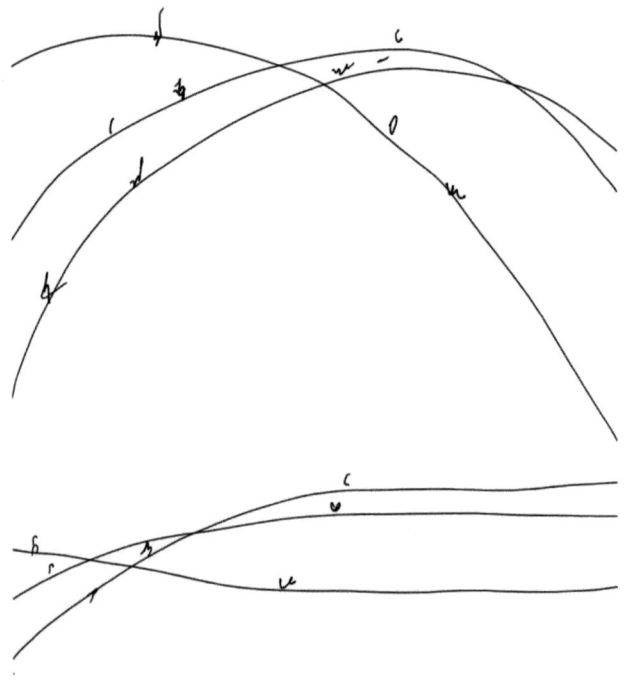

Michael Holst: Quietly Given Sublimity
Digital Drawing 2022

Epigram

The place where you are,
is the place where you should be.

We

We sleep
in the morning,
when the day
is done,
the shadows
of the night
are gone
and life
has recovered.

Woodside Writers Group
on round wooden Tables
with some undescribable holes
and protection masks,
pictures on my
smartphone.

There

There is
no reason
to worry
about
that
said
a gray
cat.
That.

The really good thing, I think

The really good thing,
I thought
is,
that up to now
no really bad things
happened
in my life.

Of course
that is not true
exactly
thinking of my teeth
and my broken arm
and the lost loves.

But compared to other fates …

… and then I think
the good thing is
that I think it is good
and that *is* really good.

The thing I love

The thing I love
about the future,
is, that no one
knows
what the future will be.

VII. Tasks

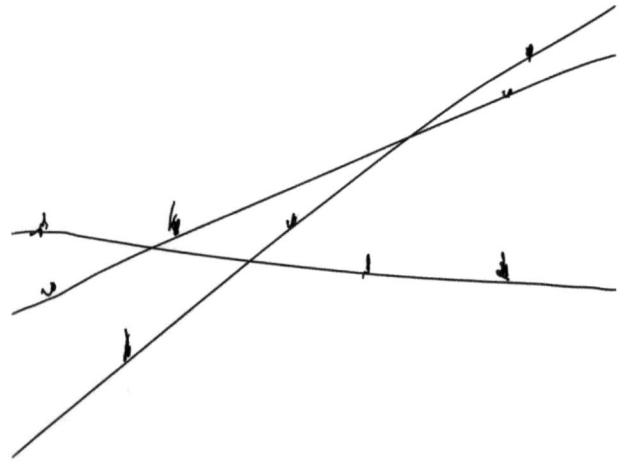

Michael Holst: New Line Studies for Paul Julius Kleiber
Digital Drawing 2022

Our work-dust can't

Our work-desk can't
always be right
or placed on the
right side.

It had to be
moved away
and the work
had gone
from the middle
of the old table
to some green
or black vases
on a window sill
in a New York
suburbs kitchen.

Period in my dreams
and line
in the towels
on the drying racks
in some planets
deserts where transparent
suns reveal their secret.

Love the eyes
that let the light
enter your boy.

The nose

The nose of the nurse
and the flattering misbelieve
of the stolen potatoes on the floor.

Of course the next
flood is not waiting
and behind the well observed
corners of madness
someone with unordinary
long hair is waiting.

Perhaps as you wait
a memory of a swimming pool
in the 41st floor of a German hotel
may come back

– touched reality –

fading.

Only

Only a banana
has been left
of the past
I've never seen.
Some branches already lost
their leavers
and the changing colors
are a mystery to those
who see them.

*About a book**

It was written
in big and mainly capital
letters.
The language
colorful
but far away
from being artistic.

The woman
of the Russian ambassador
in Spain
loved
the feeling
of having a reputation
and a daughter
that increased it.

He knew
people thought about him
in a very good way
and of course he was
a honourable man.

How can you get to know
how the story goes on
without reading the book
lying for so long now already
on the already read books
standing between the legs

of the table near
your bed.

Sleep
well.

---

*The book, the title of this poem refers to is: Carmen Boullosa: The
Book of Anna (ISBN 978-1-56689-577-4). I read a review about it
in the New York Times and purchased it. I didn't manage to read
more than the first 14 pages. I think the idea is great to follow Tol-
stoy, but then the linguistic-narrative level should be that of Tolstoy
too, and not only the first name of Tolstoy's main character should
decorate the title. And yet, or perhaps because of this, I always feel a
certain sadness when I pick up the book, always intending to go on
reading, hoping to find something of the idea that appealed to me
so much.

Remembrance

A first step
in trying to understand
the view of a horse
standing on the
self-made bookshelf
in my cologne room
looking, or better said,
focusing the view
on some pieces of
clay, a tiny collection
from my bicycle trips.

The people remain
in their dreams
outwarded in some lines
and the revelation
was not – so far –
understood.

Butterflies may need,
as you know,
some support, too.

The

The flying bodies
chains and the
tightly dropping
water drops
drops of water
on the floor
the thin oil film
on it
soon entering
the sole
of my socks
slightly feeling
like walking
on an icy ground.
Still to stop
some tracks
on the dusty surface
of the little
metallic box
on the desk.

Ask me something
dear riddle of the world.
I hope my ears
will still hear
your questions.

IIX. Lost

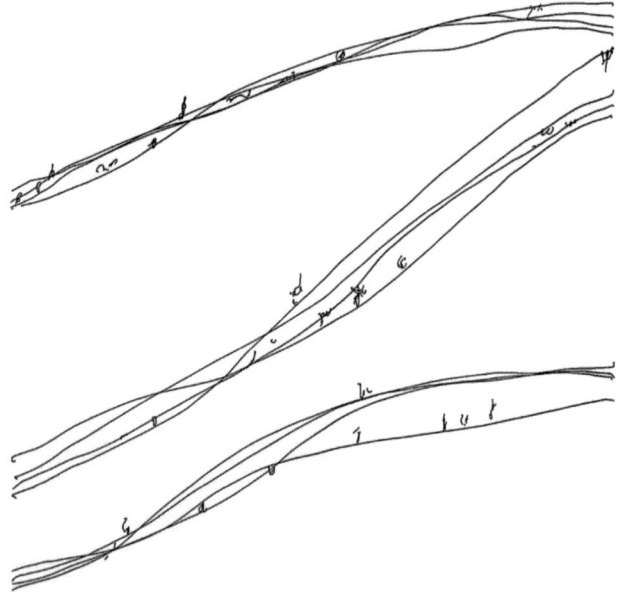

Michael Holst: The Nightingale was Lost a Few Days Ago
Digital Drawing 2022

Statement
<filled with self-consciousness>

When we tried to understand
the world
– last Friday evening,
at the end of a
sunny October –
we found the formula
very simple
and that you will understand
made us believe
that we were right
and only a really
very small period of time
before we thought
now everything will
be understood properly
and everything will be,
in the most easily
and clearest way,
understandable for
everybody with a
clear mind,
we found out
that there was
a – by the way
really very tiny –
missing step
or argument
or thought

or some part
of an idea
yet not uttered
or thought about
and this
made the whole formula,
we have to commit
useless.

We now just
know – somehow quoting Socrates –
that we don't know
anything
and,
in a quite open contrast
to Socrates
we even don't know
why and how
we don't know.

We are even
not able to feel
something like a kind
of sorrow for that.

But of course
our apologies
are written on the little
white card we
give to our visitors.

What is left

What is left of the spring
or the autumn or the leaf
that I pointed at the small
piece of wall between the
door to my dormitory and
the wardrobe corner that
was the end of a staircase.

The little liquid liar

Time has come and time has gone
lines lay on floors and carpets
and no one is seen.

Bottles empty themselves and run away
from the butterflies.

Remind me

Haven't been here
frequently or recently
and the told fairy tale
has been a lie
naturally in a world
where lies are
every days regular diet.

Only a few moments later
the very simple reality
is coming back
and I think I should
make a date
for the next volume
of my poems,
fearing they will get lost.

IX. Conscious

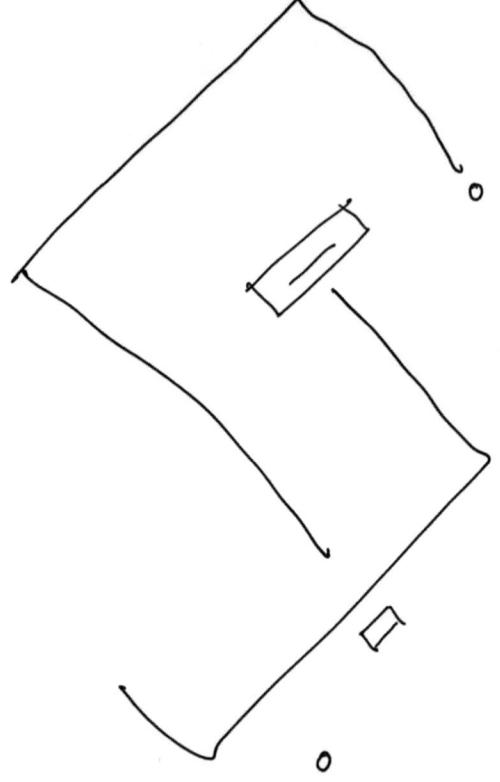

Michael Holst: The Smiling Pyramids Ground Plan Riddle
Digital Drawing 2022

My way

on my way
in my way
with my way

Marginal note:
Sometimes, really only
sometimes, I am tired
of the garbage pieces
put together with a certain,
not at all deniable, taste,
the color and form scraps
of the modern, no,
the calling itself modern,
art of the present.
They mean nothing
to me,
the blobs and arches
and the well-trodden stairs
of modernism
that no one
likes to walk on
anymore.
Walter König to his son:
„The 18th century is not present
in this store. „*
But it should be,
I think, and then I think of
the shrink-wrapped book about
Goethe's Italian journey
something like „ Journey to an
ideal country that didn't exist „**
I might have bought the book
if I could have looked inside.***

Peter, I think Peter
from the text book
of my first or second
English class
asked for some
flowers
and something to drink.

Today I would be able
to give him some water
and of course some flowers too,
though I have to admit
that I would prefer
to give them to
Helga Smith from Epping
or was she from Neustadt
and lived in Epping
as an exchange Student?
She has to be now 55 or 56
roundabout,
or do people in books
not get older?
Silly question
but quit a
difficult answer
if you are really
interested
in the truth.

But truth may be a foreign word
in today's world current languages.

My brother asked for some cups of life
and I hesitate to say what he got back.

<a few minutes later>

My brothers were caught in a delay
and David, the King, blood on his hands
was made to lead the people
but building a temple was denied.

My brother again asked
for a ship or some fish
and a riddle
behind the nearly lifted
curtains.

---

*Unintentionally eavesdropped conversation between father and son on 23.10.2020 while I was browsing the bookshelves of the wonderful bookstore of Walter König in Ehrenstraße in Cologne.

**Tiroler Landesmuseum Ferdinandeum, Assmann, P. 1. H., Pereña, H. 1. H., & Ramharter, J. 1. H. (2020). Goethes italienische Reise: Eine Hommage an ein Land, das es niemals gab = Il viaggio in Italia di Goethe : un omaggio a un paese mai esistito. Milano: Skira. ISBN 9788857244075

***Bought the book a month later after having it opened to me.

In the silent

In the silent
morning's glow
the kitchen clock
counting the time
with its steady ticks.

Why should I read

the morning post(s)
if I can take a long view
out of the window?
Why should I worry
about the world's struggles
if I am just here
at the, yes admit,
dying big river
and the, yes again admit,
dying trees.
If it is only that it,
goes, a little bit faster.
I still hesitate
but perhaps I have to say
that I enjoy it.

Yes?

Periods of the day

at night
you should sleep
at day
you should work
and all the time
you should live your dream
and stay
real.

Gratitude

for that what is
in the time passing
and passed
and what is now.

And

– and then
he reached out
to write another
chapter of
the iron curtain
story
bringing it just again
home.

Would be a
night-
mare.

The Re-flection

of a summer's
time.

X. Encounter

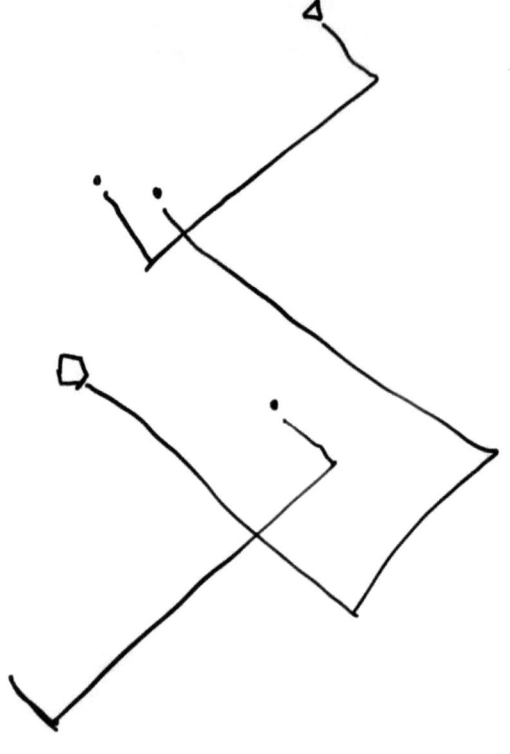

Michael Holst: Dogs Tale and Cats' Spoon
Digital Drawing 2022

For Sylvia Plath

We met in summer 1952
or perhaps 25 or 29.
I honestly have to admit
that I don't remember the year
and – sorry for that –
not the place.

Sometimes, in a certain mood,
I even wonder if we
ever meet at all.
And looking at the small stripe
of my recorded reality
I am forced to state
that we never met at all
and that the newspaper-image
was the first time, I saw you
and read your name.

But I remember some of your words
– at least some
and not the ones
read on the typograph scan
the search engine
brought on my tablet's display –
and – very certain –
I remember a smell,
the smell of that time
and when I see
for example

in the above quoted newspaper
one of these early,
slowly getting common
color photographs,
for example you, walking in Paris
and in the background
Notre Dame's façade,
darkened by the dirt of centuries passed,
I have this certain smell
in my nose,
the smell of the time
of the years
before I was born
and the freedom
of great worlds opportunities
I never got to know
as growing up in the anxious
narrowed views of my
post war time shocked parents.

I sometimes think
my life could have changed
meeting a woman like you
or one of your contemporary
getting in touch with the time
that shaped my coming in this world.
And reading this article
making this thoughts rise
I wonder what my wish
of getting in touch
with the beings expiring new

post war freedom and possibilities,
what my getting in touch with
the pre-birth-past,
means for my present being.

Es könnte aber auch
nur das Echo
einer um das Überleben
oder den Anspruch
der Kinder der Überlebenden
kämpfenden Generation sein,
im Schatten von Holocaust
und Atombombe aufgewachsen
in einer Blase der Angst
atmen lernen,
einer Blase der Angst
die mit Angst und Schrecken
die Gestalt des Schrecklichen
zum Zurückweichen bringen will,
so wie die Fratzen,
in den Fassaden
der romanischen Kirchen
die Dämonen
von dem heiligen Ort
abschrecken sollen.

But it also could be
only the echo
of a for survival
or the claim
of the survivors children
struggling generation,
in the shadow of Holocaust
and atomic bomb grown up
in a bubble of fear
learning to breathe,
a bubble of fear
that with fear and terror
the figure of the terrible
will make shrink back,
like the grotesque faces
in the facades
of the Romanesque churches
the demons
from the holy place
should scare away.

And as I struggle to decipher
the lines I find placed
with the tablets pen
under the plain
thin glass surface

I hesitate to believe
that they are characters
understandable
for anyone.
But, do they have to be?

---

*The newspaper article mentioned in the poem is: Daphne Merkin: Shifting the Focus From Sylvia Plath's Tragic Death to Her Brilliant Life, The New York Times, Oct. 27, 2020; Updated Nov. 30, 2021. In the web you can find it via the link in the QR-Code below:

The passing eye of the moment

As a view changes
on the changing things
the opposite-me
is slightly not that
that it was
a few seconds
ago.

Questions

The simple
Question
simply is,
if he or she
can convince
an audience,
his or her
or whatever,
but it has
to be
convincing.

Does it
you?

Haven't ever seen somebody being so reluctant before.

As there was no title

When sugar
wasn't sweet again

The Cow

The cow
is an apple
early in the morning
and in the evening
it is a little child
sitting on the tree's branch
in front of my office's window,
singing a song
I never heard.

And I ask you
to listen, now.

It

It is perhaps
a pair of scissors
finding its way
through mountains of papers
and the outcome
is a little monumental painting,
a collage of snippets
telling the up to now
untold story of the
world.

Being a world
creation.

The mornings

The morning's silent beauty
and some exaggerations
from an unread transcript
and some plans
with understandable lines
developing a
certainly never coming to life
future, riddle driven.

Back ground poetry

Explanations
of riddled lines
to make sure
later generations
will not understand
things different.

Or perhaps
it is only for myself
(one of my tries
to fight
forgetfulness).

XI. Truth

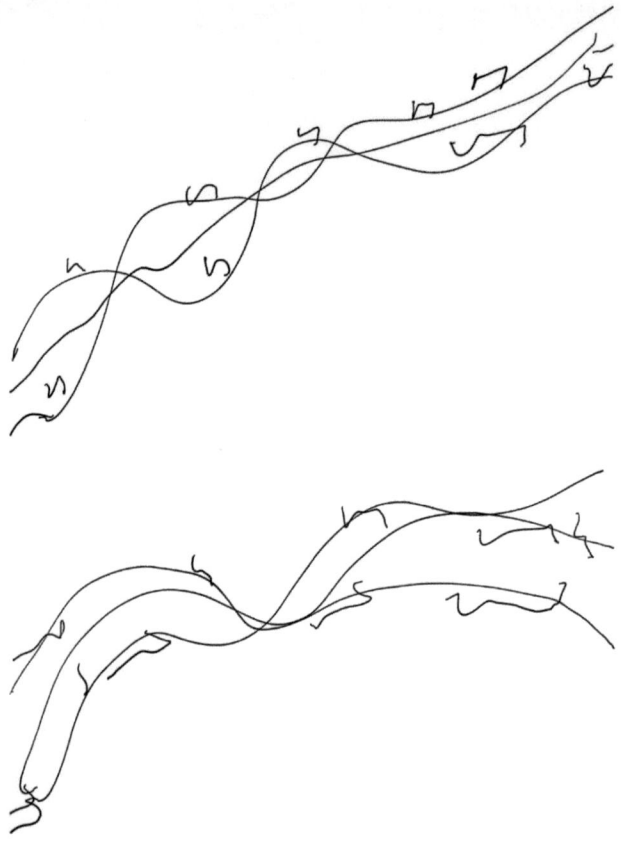

Michael Holst: Twisted Structure Lines
Digital Drawing 2022

It wouldn't be

the truth
what will be said
if we ask
what has happened
and if the question
is asked
what will be
there is no one
to give an answer,
even if he would like to.

Footprints of the future
lying in the backyard
of the past.

On a lawn

Outside
on a well cut lawn
some judges
who had left their black robes
inside, discussed
whether it would be possible
or from some point of view
at last would make sense
to pardon a cow.

The wind blew
some scraps of the conversation
over to me
and even though I didn't understand
what they were saying
and what issues
they were discussing
it occurred to me
that on the short-shorn lawn
there was no grass left
that could have been offered
to a cow.

Written on 06.12.2020, after reading an article about the possibili-
ties of a pardon or tolerating a self-pardon of US President Donald
Trump.

The interrogations

They were so shy
that they even
hesitated to look
in his face,
not to speak of looking
in the files or the accounts
so clearly documenting his
corruption and obvious
wrong doing.

They closed their eyes
just in the fear
that seeing all the defendants deeds
would show
the lie based construction
of their own lives.

They called it
impeachment
but they felt
that it impeached
themselves
for letting happen
what had happened
and so they continued
to let it happen.

A nation losing
common consensus.

And not only I ask myself
whether that can be changed
or if there is a
turning point.

Silver lies

He was
a silver
liar.

Of course everybody
knew it
but only you,
one single you
didn't get it?

There were so many
unknowing "you"
outside there
giving their money
to support the lie-story.

_____

Can a country become a lie?

_____

In Russia for example
long traditions of public lies
are promoted
sometimes there seems to be
no really big difference
between the so called Western Countries
and the authoritarian regimes
the old ones and
the newly rising.

But I think
that there still
is a difference
and it has to be seen.

Good luck
little world
at the edge.

Transkriptions Erkenntnis

The best riddles
are the unsolved.

Die Besten Rätsel
sind die ungelösten.

Life is one of them.
Das Leben ist eines davon.

The why project

The
why is it so difficult
to understand the world,
life,
my neighbor
and of course my self
project.

Understanding
really indeed is
a problem
and by the way
a key to understand
the world, myself
and life
and thought,
if of course
it is really
or in a cycle
true:
Understanding is the key
to understand.
Do you understand?

Every

Every Monday
on a morning
a usual Monday
morning
I went
gone
not known
what was
usual
usually

Public

Public
-ation
s

Some books
have been published
in winter.
Some books
have been published
before midnight.

Some books
never have been read
and at last
some should
be read.

Always Present Future

"We will go into the park,
Beatrice", the woman said
to the child,
"only for a while,
your dad has some work
to do."

The woman didn't know
that this was the last time
the child
that was in her care
saw it's father.

Shot by a hired gunman,
was the phrase in the newspaper article.

There still were some traces of blood
between the fine wood fibers
of the top of the writing desk
but nothing else told the story
of what had happened here
nearly a year ago.

This year had changed the child.

She was 14 when her father died.
Now, only one year later,
she had the face expression
of an adult woman.

The way she moved her head
when she focused on the so well known furniture,
the big mirror over the elegant chimney
and the little sofa
in the rooms left corner
that lead to the small balcony
with the iron grille.

"Who will give me back
my life?",
was the unspoken question
on her thin lips.

Underestimating the girls
determination would be
a total misunderstanding.
She knew what she wanted to do,
had a very clear vison
of what she thought
was the right thing to do.

The machine stopped.
It suddenly stopped,
and at that moment
there was no one
who was able or willing
to start it again.

The girl looked for
a screwdriver.
For a girl

wearing a 19th century dress,
that was a too much practical action.
But why stay,
in past time patterns
she thought.
We produce this picture
in the present, and:
the future is the present.

Truth

The green banana
is a yellow apple
and the things you see
are not
what they supposed to be.

Why my believe
has changed
and yours
will not be know
by anyone
is certainly
so secret
as what birds may sing
on a shiny morning
or on a late tired day.

But after all
I want to stay
at least
a few more days.

Who knows.

XII. Dream

Michael Holst: Warm Fog Trust
Digital Drawing 2022

The little lady's summer

The little lady's summer dream
was certainly a dream
and my remembrance
was still
to uncertain
to write it down
as I only indistinctly
remember what so troubled me
that afternoon
when I met her.

The sun was shining
and the bright warm light
falling through the big tall windows
of the large chamber
in her parents' home
was filled with the warmness
of her clear soft
so intensively vivid sounding
voice.

As if the dream
would be future
her words evoked
warmness in my heart,
and I asked myself
what I was actually doing,
me, the listener.

The curious

The curious modes of love
of the unknown Lilly Carter
in the early 1920th
or 1970th or even later
were told to be
an inspiration for
Henry James or Ernest Hemingway.

Routines

The routines of
the quiet Sunday morning
are still present
in the world's chaos
and I'd like to understand
a grip in the snow
on the roof
as a sign

of freedom
in an endangered
world.

Small devices

Every day some more
small device
in my hand
promising or estimated to
make my life
more comfortable.

Virtuoso gestures
to hold tablet,
mobile phone, their pens
and the torch light
from the mountain bikes handlebars
in my only two hands.

The last

I took
the last cookie
out of the box.

Of course
tomorrow
I can buy
new cookies
and all
the other things
I need
for my life.
But right now
it was the last
cookie
and as I threw
the empty box
in the corner
where I store
the old papers
and cardboard packaging
I just again
repeated in my mind
that it was
the last one,
the last.

the american

friend
on the stairs
just up on the stairs
in the bright light
of the afternoon sun
or the evening's
glow
had been
on the moon,
but the letter
i really am
waiting for
is the letter
from the first human
on the little planet
mars.

perhaps,
and from today's knowledge seen,
it never will be written.
too big are the problems there
for humans
and there are even bigger
problems to solve
here on earth.

love these humans
for dealing with really
absolutely second line problems

138

and not solving
the demands of the first line,
said one of the young gods
still being new
in the department
caring for
or better to say,
observing
life on earth.

Everything

Everything is a good idea.

In times where nothing
is done properly
everything is, or seems
to be a good idea
and it certainly is
better than doing
the old mistakes
though exactly that is
what is done.

Grip

A grip at the shoulder
from a friend
a simple gesture of support
and an impetus
for a little change
of direction
more towards the center

Screw drivers

Screw drivers make happy
is a saying no one
really knows
and perhaps
it is
not at all
a saying
even not
in the rose garden
of a broken English,
but it is
definitely
in my memory
and they really
make you happy
the special screw drivers
lying on my desk.

Just have a try
and use them.

Imagine

Imagine you are a bird.
What would you do?
: Imagine I'm a human.
[a]/: Imagine to be a human.

Imagine to be
able
to change,
a word,
a thing,
the world.

What would you
do?

The smell

of an unearned
capitalism
in the inside walls
of my dry nostrils.

We live in the dust
and the smell
of the things
we take
out of the boxes
the delivery service
drops in front of
our not left
homes.

Proverb

I don't want to sell
salad to the butcher's dog

(proverb taken from
poem № 470
in the imaginary list
of the not existing
English poems
of an unknown
German poet)

Uptugur

the bird
from ancient times
of a childhood memory
when I was new
in the world
and still connected
to the status
of creation,
the echo of
the process
that composed me
form archaic components,
and in touch
with the swinging strings
the world is made of.

... and while

and while the birds
are singing
I lost my sleep
very well knowing
that that is not
the solution.

Perhaps I should
start to make a list
of the really necessary
things to do
a very personal list
of the things
I should do
or at least
should try to do.

What's that ringing there
in my ears?
It probably will be
the heating
and I should
think of something
nice
– illusion of course –
and sleep
and thank God
for
that I am.

Jablomov

Jablomov's night
in a fight
not to win,
and no idea
how to help.

The hunters

were silent.
They lost
the track
and their confidence
was gone.
Some tried
to change
the direction.
But how can you change
something you don't have?

You

You stole
a part
of my
life,
was my first
thought.
But after a while
I found
out
that it only was
a part
and a part of it
was yours.

---

*Words in my mind after reading an article in the New York Times
about an author and her new "end-of-marriage" book.

Home

Where everything
is so perfectly
well organized
that you could
start believing
a perfect world
is possible.

(And don't forget
to take a look
at the
[of course perfectly] done
wink of the eye.)

The Wardrobes Dialogue
at the Beginning of a Sunny Day

What may I say – said the wardrobe
at the beginning of a day
when the fresh air flows through open windows
and the sun is expected to stay.

Back

Background noise
in the somehow of nowhere
behind the sound
the loudspeakers
muffled
put in the room

I want my lips to hinder
me to swallow
the salty apple slides
I read in the news
paper.

I swallowed too much.
Evening thoughts
for a rising morning.

Arguments

The difference
– by the way –
is not too big
and the *non*
in the *sense*
is as big
as it is great
whether it is smaller
or even unseen.

My believe is
gradually changing
from minute to minute
and I admit
that a lot of minutes passed
a few moments
ago.

"You can't leave
in the middle
of an argument."*

---

*One of his colleagues to Merton Densher in: The Wings of the
Dove (film, 1997), directed by Iain Softley, Screenplay by Hossein
Amini, based on "The Wings of the Dove" by Henry James.

In Short

Better then less
is more,
better than nothing
is everything

So do
everything alright.

Irritated Romance

I'd like to stay in a park
nearby nowhere castle
but the lake is empty
and the green of the lawn
will soon turn brown.

Everyone I think
is training to live
with closed eyes
and doing some
ignore exercises.

But I don't want
to get used
to kiss grey lips
and take the dust
of dying mankind
as a kind of bitter sweets.

Perhaps I'll have to.

Painting

How easy it is
to paint
an electric pig

if it doesn't look like
a mouse.

Salty sweet chocolates

An evening enjoyment
with Max Bruch's violin concerto
and some fish
on
fresh salad and tomatoes
on a toast.

May be
a recommendation.

Brilliant waters

waiting my dear,
always waiting
and in the middle of the sun
a German spelling problem
founded a few generations ago
but still alive.

We shouldn't change the water
we should love it,
it is brilliant.

Questionnaire

What will you do?
asked the young woman
sitting opposite me
in the delayed train.

What have you done?
will be the question
I have to answer
at the Last Judgment;
at last according to
some common images.

What have I done
and what will I do?
What have we done
and what will we do?
are the questions
I ask myself,
we should ask ourselves,
knowing
that there probably
very soon
will be no one
who can ask them.

The question is clear.
It's time for giving answers.
Now!

Relatives

The brother of my father
was my uncle.
Now I am the uncle
of my brothers'
son.

Questions of a nearing autumn
(or a waning summer)

I shyly asked
if I could have
the tiny box
that was now
for such a long time already
standing on
the inherited bookshelf.

I asked for it
though it already
and for a long time
was mine.

It is
not so easy
to inherit.

Under-standing

The machines didn't understand
the little butterfly
taking a seat at their tops.
They didn't recognize
the small changes
in their world
and when they finally
found out, that there was
something being different,
it was too late,
finally,
for a new start.

... for a short time

thinking of other words
and the duties
to understand
written words
and received thoughts
just with the aim
to understand
a line describing
one of the world's
various secrets.

Is there
a library accessible
where they could
be found?

The smell

The salty smell
of the old sand mills
on my lips
and in my stomach
the grumbling acid
of too much orange juice
and blueberry quark

What I was told

I was told
to be
happy
but I wasn't.
And because
I didn't know
that it was so easy
I didn't
become it.

Lines that were
brought to me
as a quotation
were taken as my own.
And being careful
was not enough.

A book

The man
who didn't
understand
the world.

The story of a
tragic illusion.

256 pages.
Book
written on demand.

The water of the fall

Falling waters
behind the living room
and on the stairs
a bride without a groom.

I think I'll have to bring
my own light
going out so late.

And some cars
find their way,
but though I don't know
I certainly wouldn't send
a photo, anyone.

Celebrities work

The landscape had to be cleaned,
some words had to be counted
and we were so sure,
that it was wrong.
But it wasn't.

We tried again,
of course with no success
but with more pleasure,
and that definitely
changed it all.

Congratulations.

Bite

In the dark and unexpected
it bit you in the neck
not the small teeth of a bat
but the future fear
well supported by the present
time being

solution

the solution is a box
a box on a shelf
somewhere in a cabinet
it is the box
that is the solution
not what is in the box

solution box
box solution

Some proud games

We had a story written
in clear readable letters
and a wing of a green bottom line
for a while
was the example and explanation
for nearly everything.
I felt
and I certainly was sure,
that it was impossible
to write about war
when it was so present.

Perpetual Writings

for month and nothing
in a struggle of nonunderstanding
we left for the see
but our maps were broken
and no one able to read them.
Please do not,
I said,
always repeat the same
bla bla bla
even if it is
di tschi bon ta wei
which no one understands
my good God
mentioned the father.

Tea

The tea of bitterness
was sweet
in the boiled water bubbles
and Peter, or was it Betty
wondered if someone can read
a coffee table book
while drinking tea
especially if it's light green.

Fire Engines

Fire engines are always
red.

Questions and Answers

Q: Can we survive?
A: Yes.
Q: Will we survive?
A: No.

And now
room for
discussions.

No saints

There are
no saints
available
at this table
please change
your place
or go to another
restaurant,
was the unbelievable
message
in spring
when we left
for new
vacations.

Nobody
did look
for saints
and that made
it even more
difficult to understand
the angels word.
But we were sure
that it was
an angel
speaking to us
though
we didn't know

where to look
to see him.

In fact
I was quite sure
that he wasn't there
but that was
what made me
even more sure to believe
in his existence.
Please don't apologize
please not.

A past nights fairy tale

In the windy storms of yesterday
my darling wrote a letter
in the windy storms of yesterday
my darling made me laugh

With the drowning storms
I flew away
grey water waves
knocking at my door
tearing down my homes walls
and no one took my hand

In the windy storms of yesterday
my darling got lost
my hopes flew away
an no one brought them back

It is my duty
to change the world
an angel says
but I don't know
if I could bear
the angels words
and its demands

It is all a little bit
too strong
and from an
old-fashioned time

As I say good by
to this mood
I say good by
to this my world

Snake

Mister Morlay was ill.
He didn't know
what illness it was
that so suddenly
hurt him.

The doctor said
it was a creeping disease
and that it started
a long time ago.

There were some memories,
that he mentioned it earlier
but he was not sure at all
and now it was
something new
and action had
to be taken.

But no one took action,
nothing happened.
And that is
– he thought –
what will happen
now.

A stone was thrown
on a tank.
People were killed,

their bodies stayed
unburied,
but that was not
the main problem,
between the grass roots.

Someone was dreaming
of a snake
that never occurred
at the right time
in the story
and for some unknown reason
no one asked it
to leave.

I wonder why.

Developing

The story
of the reconstruction
of the tragic life
of Harry P.

I wonder,
if there is
a connection
to my life
beyond coincidental
concurrence.

I want
to understand
what makes it
so fascinating
for so many
people.

Something like an equation

The rich are rich,
and: The poor are poor.

Though I never experienced
what it means to be rich,
I also have to admit,
that I never experienced poverty.

The rising question is,
whether the one or the other
is a deprivation.

Time for a walk

Do I have
time for a walk,
now
on a Thursday evening?

There is a forest
in front of my door
and the weather
is fine
after some very heavy
rain showers.

Am I so busy
this evening,
is there so much
to do
that I really can't go
for a walk?

In former times

In former times
we were late
when the train arrived
and we didn't know
where to go
in the empty station.

Today
it took us some time
to find out,
that we were tired
and that there was
a small chap in the nail
always snagging in the surface
of the cloth.

And my question is:
Is there anything to stay?

There have

been people
dreaming
to a certain extend
of a world
beyond the thoughts,
more than
the well-known story
of the apple
and the snake.

Certainly unknown
but well to find
there has
in the struggle of understanding and misunderstanding
to be
something more
as here is.

Long List

The long list
of ideas I never had,
could be added by
the long list
of things I never did,
and the long list
of things that never happened
and never will happen.

It could become an entry
in the list of the lists
I never made.

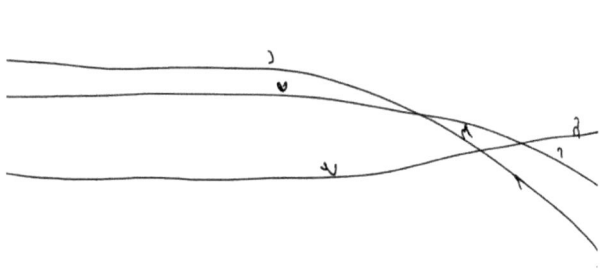

Content

IV. Reflections

V. Bitter

VI. Hope

VII. Tasks

IIX. Lost

IX. Conscious

X. Encounter

XI. Truth

XII. Dream

Index of Poem Titles

Index of Poem Beginnings

Books, Articles, Films and Radio Plays

quoted [Q], mentioned [M] or referred to [R]

Boullosa, Carmen: The Book of Anna, Coffee House Press 2020, ISBN 978-1-56689-577-4; [M] p. 51, 60, 76.

ENGLISH Ausgabe G, Band 1 A für das 5. Schuljahr an Gymnasien und Gesamtschulen. 1. Auflage, 3. Druck 1980, Cornelsen-Velhagen & Klasing GmbH & Co, Berlin 1978; [M] p. 92.

Goethe, Johann Wolfgang: Italienische Reise, Textkritisch durchgesehen von Erich Trunz, Kommentiert von Herbert von Einem, C. H. Beck, München 1981, ISBN 978 3 406 61139 1; [M] p. 91.

Gontscharow, Iwan: Oblomow. German radio play (WDR) based on the Novel "Oblomov" by the Russian author Iwan Gontscharow, translation: Helmut Peschina, edited for the radio play by Helmut Peschina, music: Henrik Albrecht, directed by Leonhard Koppelmann. First broadcast 13.10.2003; [R] p. 148.

Irving, John: The Hotel New Hampshire, Jonathan Cape, London 1981, ISBN 9780224019613; [R] p. 27.

James, Henry: The Wings of the Dove. Constable, London, August 30, 1902; Scribner's, New York, August 21, 1902; [R] p. 154.

Menke, Marcellus M., and Holst, Michael A.: The President who became a Wardrobe. Ludwig Miller Kronberg Edition № 1, ISBN 9783751997126; [R] p. 152.

Merkin, Daphne: Shifting the Focus From Sylvia Plath's Tragic Death to Her Brilliant Life. The New York Times, Oct. 27, 2020; Updated Nov. 30, 2021; [M] p. 103.

Savage, Charlie: Can Trump Pre-emptively Pardon Allies or Himself? Clemency Power, Explained. The New York Times, Jan. 20, 2021; [R] p. 118.

Shakespeare, William: Sonnet 116; [R] p. 31.

The Wings of the Dove (film, 1997), directed by Iain Softley, Screenplay by Hossein Amini, based on "The Wings of the Dove" by Henry James; [Q] p. 154.

Tiroler Landesmuseum Ferdinandeum, Assmann, P. 1. H., Pereña, H. 1. H., & Ramharter, J. 1. H. (2020). Goethes italienische Reise: Eine Hommage an ein Land, das es niemals gab = Il viaggio in Italia di Goethe : un omaggio a un paese mai esistito. Milano: Skira. ISBN 9788857244075; [M] p. 93.

Persons Mentioned

Bruch, Max; German Composer (1838 – 1920); p. 158.

Carter, Lilly; Belgian feminist and pedagogue (1865 – 1937); p. 134.

David, King; biblical character; p. 93.

Densher, Merton; fictional character in: The Wings of the Dove (1997, film), directed by Iain Softley, Screenplay by Hossein Amini. Based on "The Wings of the Dove", novel by Henry James; p. 154.

Goethe, Johann Wolfgang; German poet, playwright, novelist, scientist, statesman, theatre director, and critic (1749 – 1832); p. 91.

Hemingway, Ernest; American novelist, short-story writer, and journalist (1899 – 1961); p. 134.

Jablomov; wrongly remembered name of fictional character from WDR German radio play "Oblomov" based on the Novel by the Russian author Iwan Gontscharow, translation: Helmut Peschina, edited for the radio play by Helmut Peschina, music: Henrik Albrecht, directed by Leonhard Koppelmann, First broadcast 13.10.2003; p. 148.

James, Henry; American-born British author (1843 – 1916); p. 134, 154.

Karenina, Anna; fictional character, eponymous protagonist in Leo Tolstoy's novel; p. 51.

König, Walter; German bookseller and publisher (*1939); p. 91.

Plath, Sylvia; American poet, novelist, and short-story writer (1932 – 1963); p. 103.

Potter, Harry; fictional character; eponymous protagonist in the Novels by J. K. Rowling; p. 183.

Smith, Helga; fictional character in: ENGLISH Ausgabe G, Band 1 A für das 5. Schuljahr an Gymnasien und Gesamtschulen. 1. Auflage, 3. Druck 1980, Cornelsen-Velhagen & Klasing GmbH & Co, Berlin 1978; p. 92.

Socrates; classical Greek philosopher (470 – 399 BC); p. 84.

List of Illustrations

Digital drawings by Michael Holst

Michael Holst created the digital drawings in spring 2022 when he got a first copy of the poems.

futurely existing books

Book written on Demand

www.buchmanufaktur.m4art.de

Marcellus M. Menke
Wie Musik
für die Augen
zum Lesen
Geschenkte Gedichte
Köln 2015 • ISBN: 9783837021738

Marcellus M. Menke
Für einige Augenblicke
Gedichte
Köln 2016 • ISBN: 9783741256493

Marcellus M. Menke
Von innen heraus
Gedichte
Köln 2017 • ISBN: 9783744852227

Marcellus M. Menke
Im Zeitstrom
Gedichte
Köln 2018 • ISBN: 9783748171058

Marcellus M. Menke
Liebkosung
Wie eine zugeflogene Melodie
Gedichte
Köln 2019 • ISBN: 9783750416246

Marcellus M. Menke
Konstruktion
Gedichte
Köln 2022 • ISBN: 9783756223237

editionHIC<

Le Tschen

Wie man die Radioaktivität überlebt

Siebenunddreißig mikroskopische
Erzählungen in drei Büchern

Aus dem Japanischen von
Masahiro Miyamoto

Mit Nachworten
von Marcellus M. Menke

Köln 2015

ISBN: 9783734791277

Marcellus M. Menke (Hrsg.)

Zukunftsgeschichten

Texte von
Michael Quant,
Alexandra Kirschbaum,
Brian T. Ballmoor und
Pascal-David Dombeaux

Köln 2017

ISBN: 9783743159266

editionHIC<

Marcellus M. Menke

Im hinteren Teil
des Himmels

ausgewählte Gedichte
aus 27 Jahren

Köln 2020

ISBN: 9783752896855

Marcellus M. Menke

Zwischenbuch

Gedichte, Grafiken und Buchtitel

Durchgesehen und neu zusammengestellt auf
der Basis der Erstausgabe von 2005

Köln 2017

ISBN: 9783744812580

editionHIC<